TRILLIUM

Poems by

Richard Foerster

Richard Foerster (signature)

BOA Editions, Ltd.　❧　Rochester, NY　❧　1998

LC #: 97–74817
ISBN: 1–880238–61–6 trade paperback
ISBN: 1–880238–62–4 limited edition

First Edition
98 99 00 01   7 6 5 4 3 2 1

Publications by BOA Editions, Ltd.—
a not-for-profit corporation under section 501 (c) (3)
of the United States Internal Revenue Code—
are made possible with the assistance of grants from
the Literature Program of the New York State Council on the Arts,
the Literature Program of the National Endowment for the Arts,
the Lannan Foundation, the Sonia Raiziss Giop Charitable Foundation,
the Eric Mathieu King Fund of The Academy of American Poets,
as well as from the Mary S. Mulligan Charitable Trust,
the County of Monroe, NY,
and from many individual supporters.

Cover Design: Geri McCormick
Cover Art: Mary Vaux Walcott, "Snow Trillium (*Trillium Grandiflorum*),"
watercolor on paper, 1923. National Museum of American Art,
Smithsonian Institution, Gift of the Artist.
Manufacturing: McNaughton & Gunn, Lithographers
BOA Logo: Mirko

BOA Editions, Ltd.
Alexandra Northrop, Chair
A. Poulin, Jr., President & Founder (1976–1996)
260 East Avenue
Rochester, NY 14604

Again for DR

Contents

I

Marginalia   13
The Clearing   15
The News   16
The Failure of Similes   17
Millennial Song   18
Wood Ducks at Yaddo   19
Fiddleheads   20
Barberry   21
Judas Trees   22
Cantus   23
The White Orchids   24
Evening Game   25
A Rogue Wave   26
Autumn Nightfall   28
Garden After Frost   29
An Absurdity   30
Icebound   32

II

Holyrood Abbey   37
The Traffic Between   38
Tulips   40
Masks   41
Nettle   42
The Rock Doves   43
Northern Lights   44
Remembering the Garden   45
Poe in the Bronx   46

Out of Grimm   47
Vacant Lot   50
Trilliums   52
Plenitude   54
Spring Peepers   55
At the Cove   56
Isolation Ward   57
On Lexington Avenue   59

III

Emily Dickinson in Boston, 1864–65   63
Odonata   65
From Hawthornden Castle   67
Little Homages   69
Invitation to a New Year   71
Broth   72
Constable's Cloud Studies   73
In the Moment   74
Even in the Touch   75
Valentines   76
Geological Survey   77
Brueghel's Harvesters   78
Ant World: The Leaf-Cutters   80
A Tetradrachm of Alexander the Great   82
Snorkeling   83
Butterfly Farm   84
The Book Cover   85

Notes   88
Acknowledgments   90
About the Author   92

TRILLIUM

I

Marginalia

At first, in Catherine's *Hours of the Cross,*
the marginalia snared me: the swirling tendrils
of invention and intricate gilt, the spiky leaves
and incongruous fauna among the half-familiar
blooms—page after page of extravagant treasure
hunts on the outskirts of drama where a child could spend
his sickbed hours wandering with a Peterson's Guide
and gather along the way the simplest lore:
blue columbines like pleated lanterns, or the small
rockets of nightshade—the balm and bane of a distant
pharmacology growing among fever-stale blankets.

And afterwards, during idle prowlings
through the brittle leaves of a *Webster's First*
that my father had hauled out of someone's trash
for me, the thingness of words took shape
and shifted, flew up like a flock of doves
[< L. *columbinus*], or clawed the air,
mighty and Latinate [*Aquilegia* < *aquila*]—
until I wondered how that woman of privilege
passed the minutes of her silent devotions,
caught, as she must have been, beyond words
in that florid net of indirection. For how rarely

now I wish to struggle back to here,
where one of Catherine's Christs, blindfolded,
is made to sit squarely at the center
of things while thugs with staves impress a ring
of thorns deeper through his pliant scalp.
These five encircling men who slap and jeer
still too easily pass for neighbors. And in the *Real-*

politik of governing, this man whose robe
spills like blood upon the parquetry
must have been a minor inconvenience—
and yet it seems a necessary way of seeing:

the brutal moment lavish as the world,
its logic hammered out like filigree.

The Clearing

Always in that clearing
the oaks are black with crows
and I can't be certain
my presence starts it
but something catches like
a fuse, and the branches seethe
until the air grows raucous
with calling crows. First one,
then another, now all
stretch into brief grace
then oar up into a spiral-
ing choir, into such teasing
synchroneity, just approaching
then skirting a pattern.

Far below and minuscule
under that disarming blue
circle of light, I watch them,
charred bits in a whirl-
wind of logic, beyond grasp
of cause or destiny, beyond
delight or grief. Their flight,
I tell myself, has nothing
to do with me, and that widening
echo, even when it falls
together a moment, orchestral,
has nothing to do with me,
though it sounds at times fearsome
and something like a name.

The News

filters through thin gauze, like the dark
     Kenyan brew we crave each morning.
Some days, it's a less-than-pure snort from Peru,
     the minim of atropine applied
with a pipette to widen the eyes. Like a distillate
     of mashed ylang ylang and amber-
gris, it's the foul refined for wearing in
     polite society, the minted
breath we bear to the office, the whitened teeth
     with which we face the world—how else
could we endure it, even secondhand?

The Failure of Similes

In one image of the camps, the snow sifts down
like lime . . . or should it be the other way around?
Mere words now tumble like . . . corpses, like . . .
windy sacks in which the soul once sang.

You might have heard them somewhere
before they bloated in those earthen wombs.
And still we pile them higher and curse the stench
that rises from the cargohold of history.

Why can't we close that gash? *O Adonai*,
some shouted (it should have wrung the sky of color).
And now *Allah, Allah*—all the names empty
toward heaven—as tongues blister in the flames.

Millennial Song

for two voices

Sparrow, sing to me today—
a bomb has blown away
the heads of children—
sing the fixed notes
that prophets heard
before they cried for blood.

Sing longer, louder, this
valley to the next, over
the whine of teamsters' rigs,
enlist the throats of all
your kind, and sing the end
of this and this and this.

Wood Ducks at Yaddo

A small, gaudy mandarin,
the male paddles Katrina's ink-
dark lake, its skittish potentate,
eyeing left then right, beyond
the waning moon-white shelf
of winter ice, some secure perch
and hollow where he'll propose
the nest. His mate, meanwhile,
quite understated in her powder-
blue Egyptian makeup, pirouettes
in a spotlit ellipse of morning
light, slipping through the oaks
as if on cue. —I stand aside

in a shadow, like those peering elders,
seduced by the beauty they plotted
for days to encounter. What does it matter,
this one more tick on my life
list of wonders? The birds court
like toys, little corybants pricking
their feathers high in a script-
ed ritual. The unerring spring
that spurs them coils to the breaking
point, and is then . . . released.
O Katrina, your children dead,
did you cry, like me, to walk here
and see such splendid mockery?

Fiddleheads

Only the first scrolls inscripted
with the long winter's undeciphered
lore, only the tight-harnessed
coils volting up fully
charged from peaty earth would do:

tiny crosiers straining to hook
the sky; spring's furled lace-
wings before the sun had a chance
to spirit them with flight. Arrested

potential I demanded with each
flick of my pruning knife, not
woodland crofts feathered wide
in August with spore-laden tracery.

How the future seemed to lie
there before me, curled and delectable.
Already the virgin oil sizzled
in my mind till I was sure
the skillet would whisper hosannas.

Barberry

All week they've come,
honeybees and hornets,
wasps and great bumblers.

This morning they swung
like electrons through pelt
and patter of sudden rain.

They even drone in this moonlight.
Their obsession obsesses me:
the allure of the barberry's

hidden thorns, its vagrant shoots,
the blood it draws, pale blooms
so plain and microscopic. Why them

when May is torching greater fires?
In their almost-dark, one might imagine
the bees dipping into paradise.

The faintest scent drifts
even now on the indifferent
air across my bed, this sagging

coracle I've tried to steer
through so many other nights
toward that landfall I seek and dread.

Judas Trees

Is this the emblem for betrayal:
a swath of fire igniting
every limb, these garnet exhalations?

Theirs is not a color
for repentence, for the inevitable,
perfunctory kiss. They rival

the dogwood's luminous pride.
Who hung that traitor's burden
here? The mere incidental

radiance should be enough
for me to risk the clamber
up this leaf-slick hill,

and stand among them
saying *redbud, cercis,*
saying *breath-of-love,* if I can.

Cantus

Not this smoke, this spent wick, but the pale
taper of his body inching down
while the bed-chart fattened with history . . .

not the facts of conquest, but the invisible
hosts riding the air, those eager settlers
on unspoilt lands . . . I never imagined so many

would stake claims and cultivate their small
estates, would give thanks, then slash and burn . . .
no, not the hardened black crust

that had been his ears, but the way his fingers
shuddered to caress the lobes . . . like piano keys . . .
no, not that aquarium room, its unmusical hiss

of filtered air, but the ulcerous curves tattooing
themselves like prisoners' trophies to his limbs,
the deadman's feet he teetered on, the withered

sex and opium-songs of the loreleis
I never heard as his eyelids sank and rose,
the unsettling composure like a washed-up treasure

he tried to share . . . no, not that parting, but
the embrace I couldn't give . . . no . . . not this
death but the dying.

The White Orchids

They do not use the air
      as swans do, though furiously winged.
This is how we'd like souls to rise:
      a weathered clay bowl knotted
with moss, the end table fixed
      in a suitable light ...
then always this urge that's taught us,
      toward immutable white,
this flock of absences, high and far
      from the grieving forest.

Silly really, like a Calder
      someone's immobilized,
but the indelible ink of this letter
      I've read and reread tonight
insists on opposites, on my climbing
      that narrow green stair
where those orchids pose—like a corps
      de ballet—as something unreal,
yet fierce with grace,
      and riveting.

Evening Game

We sat along the sturdy planks,
beneath the slow dissolve of a summer
dusk—two tiers of choirs cheering
their players on in the holy counter-
point of small-town rivalry.

And the cleat-dust rose to our lips
as we prayed for the stolen run
or sharp crack, the meteoric
arc that would send us finally
home. But the innings posted

across the board lined up like eggs
at an equinox, poised on end
in a perfect balance stretching, before
we knew to be amazed, 0
to 0 toward where the sun had set.

A Rogue Wave

This morning near my house, a wave swept up
a child from the rocks as she played. Soon all

the town's trawlers were pacing the sea's
long corridor, like family anxious for a ransom call.

Such a tiny window remained open at the end,
where the sun's needles made the sky flow red.

But we stayed, as if prayers could have sailed beyond
the unrelenting moan of the harbor horn. And later,

the air became glutted awhile with the earthy
stench of shells that the storm had washed

upshore and splayed across the rocks—innumerable
as the gathering gulls. So many wings

soared against those stony clouds. The ocean takes
its time. It yields, but somehow we hope for more:

to abstract from its surface the dream-
puncturing fact—the happenstance that can make

a mother, straitjacketed with fear, half-curse
the chantey of the waves that must bring

all loved ones home. And the gulls, as if to mock us
by example, waddled among the rich debris,

undeterred by grief. —I confess, I was hauled up
in their reverie as they rose with the few unbroken

quahogs razored in their bills and let them drop,
before their own plummet to a squabbling feast.

And when the sunlight finally clotted into black
and all but one boat came lumbering to port

and the birds departed for shelter against dark
and this night of neighbors sobbing, what was left

beyond the buoys seemed depthless as a stage, its scenery
struck, lit only by a klieg-lamp's narrow gaze.

Autumn Nightfall

In the vacant lot, amid jewelweed,
my sick dog sniffs out her pleasure
and relief while I wait and strangely

think of lust. Everywhere hidden
in the yellowed leaves, aging suitors
are bowing rusty serenades.

A few monarchs settle then flicker distract-
edly among the blooms, their tiny minds
even now struck through with longing

for their one flight south. Across the cove
the windows of the empty summer homes
burst with momentary flame. What passion

can sustain this embrace, can keep it
from uncurling into seamless dark? Curse
these dervishes of begetting, the asters'

acetylene blue, the whole fiery wheel of words
if all is but this line strung from here
to there, like a run for an old spayed bitch.

Garden After Frost

I enter it like a sickroom, breathing
      staunched against the shock
straining up to greet me . . . like a loved one
      still harboring hope.

Gangrenous rot. The impetiginous bloom.
      Only yesterday candelabras
blazed at every window, but now
      these useless shards, guttered wax

in clumps, wasps reeling in stupor,
      the morning's rasp of rusted
hinges, and yet the seed pods snap like castanets,
      with impulsive largesse. And there,

two ruby-throats quaver at the trumpet-vine,
      sipping what I must drink
each day with all my senses—draughts of desire,
      such meager parting tastes.

An Absurdity

His paranoia gripped us in its fist
till we agreed, gasping, then in tears,

to guarantee we'd watch his body meet
the flames intact. He'd heard of undertakers

selling off the hearts and lungs, any
reusable parts, then packing off what's left

to student labs. This man, whose heart had pumped
butter, whose lungs had bellowed nicotine,

died in fear of a pharaoh's afterlife
spent in endless litigation—a stranger

in the courts of paradise, squabbling
to regain his missing guts. And so

we watched them haul his body in and lift
the cardboard lid. His rigorous flesh lay pure

as an ivory tusk beneath the cotton sheet.
His face was left as he had wished, untouched

by any embalmer's sleight of hand—half-
amazed, the mouth agape as if stunned

by an unexpected kiss. What could we do
but stand there a moment, sobbing

at the horror of our love, before one of us
with sense gave the signal to begin.

Icebound

Nine below and each window's
a milky caul or cataract,
the sea a leaden caldron

steaming, each molecule
of light a spike against
whatever bit of skin's

left exposed. The house-
beams snap, brittle
as porous bones. Cold

paradoxes! Billions
somewhere stretch their arms
like stamens toward the sun.

This oneness, at-oneness—the very
idea rebounds like a self-
referential echo inside a cave,

ringing a moment everywhere
with *I am here . . . here*
before the inevitable fade.

The shade-drawn room,
the blankets' rumpled warmth,
the dog snoring at your side—

all the comforts drain
through cracks you cannot stop.
And the perceptible chill invades.

in memoriam JM

Holyrood Abbey

No guidebook description prepares for this
sudden gutted emptying to sky. A church
all husk. A walled perimeter barely defining
a hallowed space. And you must walk on names
of the dead, island to island in a shallow sea
of yesterday's weather, snickering
or discomfited at the irony of being
well-heeled. And in the unglassed east, a stencil—
a high, skeletal arch of quatrefoils and twelve
airy rectangles—rises where apostles may once have
intervened. Outside, in steady succession,
tour buses belch and grind away. They leave
an unsettled peace, too many imaginings
of clashing swords and righteous rabble,
and of the magpie centuries stripping faith
to faith's essentials—all the hard knocks
and the final coup, an act of God no less,
that peeled the roof away like paper.
It makes you suspect the martyrs to this place
woke into some harsher light, clutching
what certainty they still possessed
like a fragment of the cross.

The Traffic Between

. . . temendo no 'l mio dir li fosse grave,
infino al fiume del parlar mi trassi.

Like a priest in the shadowed confidence
of his confessional, the cabbie eased
one shoulder back against the plexiglass divide,
and urged the question through: *Have you*
accepted Jesus as your personal savior?

The man was too sincere for me to laugh
out loud; still, I swallowed hard, trying
to ignore the white noise that had been drawling
from his radio all along—a thorazine haze
direct from Jesus, Inc. *Can't say I have,*

I almost said, but didn't want to condemn myself
to his mercy for thirty-three blocks of midtown traffic.
For a while, his eyes seemed to linger in the rearview
where he'd strung a crucifix on a chain. It swayed
erratically, a pendulum jarred from its course,

over a small gilt frame with snapshots
of his wife and child. Beside it, a plastic pair
of praying hands, glued firm, was wreathed at the base
with a strand of worry beads. *Is there hope?*
I thought and turned my head to the motley stir

of shopfronts snailing past. Soon I was lining up
my old defensive arguments—like flintlock muskets
in humid weather. I wanted to tell him that long ago
I knelt on green slopes charged with prayer's transforming
lights, that I believed I could glimpse a face behind the scrim

of each leaf I peeled from the tablet of days on my wall.
I wanted to tell him of my sadness at waking
finally to the treadle-sounds of doctrines being honed
into axe-heads. How could I convince him that this
is how death first entered the world—through certain

faith and obedience—that the words of preachers
flow down through history like unappeasable magma,
that women can fester on the fullness of life
and the souls of children starve even faster
than flesh? This is the body

of facts that faith must swallow whole. But what
of Fr. Pelletier who tongued me in the sacristy
before saying Mass? This I would declare, and more,
in one extravagant elegy, in salvos more offensive
than evasive, and yet, when my eyes drifted back

to engage the cabbie's, I knew he was thinking,
But what's all that to do with Jesus? Is He any less
because of the sins of hypocrites? And when at last
we approached the destination, he broke the silence
matter-of-factly: *When the rapture comes,*

you know, you'll be left in the back seat
without a driver. Then where will you be?
I summoned words as best I could and wore a mock-
victorious smile: *Right here, I guess. Right here.*
Then fumbled with the fare and struggled out.

Tulips

They are the breathing that passes
for contentment, that passes into longing
after the long climb out of darkness.

See how they dance now
in our seraglio, flinging about
unblemished arms in the sun,

taunting us with their uncaring.
We attend but dare not touch
what we can't possess.

If they were Fabergé, fired
into a hardness beyond life,
we could endure fingering them

over and over for all our days.

Masks

It's our pure abandon you covet: to don the false-
hood of a fabulist, give credence to the bald lie,
and bare a face that's wholly surface, pierced only by
the eyes; to wear the dark in daylight, like a secret
pinned to a sleeve, and leer or scowl or glare at the world
with rigid composure. Like us, you'd float serenely
as a smile fired into the arctic white of porcelain
or wander through crowded nights in the leathery hide-
and-seek of anonymity. Beloved ghosts, totems
sprung from dreams, we pass for exoskeletons that shape
the soft core of your insecurities. Perfect flesh
of the imagination, we wake each day unchanged,
true, and unabsolved. We are your disembodied selves.

Nettle

Nothing binds me to you though I've watched
     you longer than I care, fording
         our green sea—thigh-deep

and head-strong. Must it always be magic
     and majesty, violet blazes
         in the swamp, blasts of way-

side gold? You should know
     we are self-serving to a fault
         and sow only to reap the humblest

immortality. Why must I instruct you
     one by one? Haven't you seen
         who attends, listened to their hymns,

prickling and mystical? Then touch.
     My pain is small as things go.
     And necessary.

The Rock Doves

Three years I commuted across the Tappan Zee, my route
never varied, just the larger reel of the seasons,
the Hudson's broad march depending on the tide,
leaf-bud and fall, the weather's caress or curse.

I aspired, and barely saw the agitated lights, the river-
wide canyon eroding beneath me, my wife
turning her back at the shore. I walked my tightrope
dreams each day, blindfolded for death-

defying routines. And so that day at my exit,
when I spotted a pair of rock doves—the kind I'd learned
to scorn as flying rats—I dismissed the metallic shimmer
rising toward me, the odd tableau they formed

against the trafficked curb: One lay dead,
windshield smashed, though gusts from passing
cars fussed with the feathers, or perhaps dropped there
when the rusted springwheels of its heart wound down.

It mattered little—and yet I noticed the mate, frozen
in the dumb, expectant posture of a question:
one well-deep eye cocked skyward; the other
drinking darkness from the ground. Was then

the answer rang out sharp and shrapnel-sudden.

Northern Lights

Late summer heat . . .
cicadas in the dark.
What was soft, jagged.

The russet glow behind
the trees blackened,
and branches coalesced

into curves of nervework.
Mosquitoes sang
veni, veni—eleven years

our porch chairs creaked
while the stars sparked
pizzicati and we eased back

out of speech. And so when,
in that sudden enveloping awe,
sheets of aurora flamed the sky,

why was I aghast at the silence,
at those greens and blues
that settled so gently upon us?

Remembering the Garden

Like friends who sat whole evenings and spoke
little, but nonetheless imparted their entire selves

and melded to one alone, but not alone—
so with us, the garden silent

by nature and we by design, while swifts
twirled in the windless dusk.

Azaleas, irises, columbines—glints
in the twilight like facets

of a compound eye—so distilled the fading
panoply of light that each petal

incandesced, gave to me a burning
vision of the world, and I—I wondered

what essence it caught of me? What flicker
of me would reside after I had gone,

who would have sustained that calm
through the separate nights I learned to bear?

Poe in the Bronx

1846–47

Here the dream turned Gothic
and the scintillant blade his imagination
had held aloft for years began to swoosh past,

its arc broad as a smirk. Whose face
did he glimpse then, descending?
Whose wild and ghastly eyes cut through

those nights at Fordham, like contagion?
Yes, a body can bleed for years
and a mattress sag like a trough

yet leave a thirst unslaked. Whatever ropes
bound him to her—"Sissy," "my dear Heart"—
they never frayed before those walls reddened

finally and the rats of conscience skittered
off for bleaker depths. He languished,
dear reader, through that summer's long

vermilions, into the starved lights
of winter—waiting for that ill-
defined "discordant hum" in his story's

ultimate paragraph, for that army of salvation
to amass somewhere beyond the cottage gate
and begin its welcome, grim advance.

Out of Grimm

1. Crone

Because mirrors are duplicitous, she breaks them
and lets the rising lava of resentment
overflow her heart and features. It hardens

like a wart on her nose. So we avert our gaze
to the pavement, but she's affronted, marks
names in her scripted maze of curses, plots

perfection in revenge: She curdles the cream-
y youth till his love's soured to lust; the maiden
he'd have, she suspends in the air-

less bubble of virginity. Her mind runs
athwart: She'd bring the city down, set
the church aflame; she'd make us knit from brambles

a wedding gown, quaff her steamy potions
of undying faithfulness—till we awake, squinting
at the unveiled image of ourselves.

2. Gnome

Confined till dark to a dark
confused with evil, she squats
bare-bellied beneath the barrel-
vaulted bridge of our dreaming.

She squeezes through from the core,
tireless in her scaling of earth's
crevices. She waits for us
by the brook's disjointed syllables,

her eyes fixed on the gullied
path we've worn with our tiger-
pacing. What must she think,
seeing us pause each night,

dumb with wonder, to stare
up toward the hollow
of that farther roof, beyond
the touch of her hands? What

unfathomed escape, what
hidden way could she offer
should she grab us by the heels
and bid us follow down?

3. Frau Trude

The forest cups her house like hands in prayer; no
       one chances by who has not searched for years.
Our hunger's the banquet she'll prepare for us,
       till our growling bellies hush as after-
smoke unbraiding from her hearth. Here the hunter
       sleeps in his moss-green skin and hears
the grazing hooves approach, the grouse nesting close.
       Here the butcher can disappear in crimson
dreams of remorse, then leach a death through every pore.
       And the charcoal-burner, sooty as the new
moon above the courtyards of the rich, can dance
       naked till dawn. And we who press
our noses to her window, despite the best advice
       against godless things, have seen our eyes
blaze back at us in the glass, yet could not turn away.

Vacant Lot

again at dusk

No doubt an oversight, a developer's glitch
in the subdivision's plan, left this "ditch,"

as my neighbor calls it, this bit of waste
too small for a house, which my study windows face.

All up and down our street the lawns are cut
and watered, gardens cleared of weeds, but

this unclaimed field escapes our tyranny—
a parcel left to shifting chance, a sea

of yellow rape, far from any pasturage;
then nearer, straps of lilies, discordant blasts

of orange clarions asserting a long-
forgotten gardener's claim, her sure, strong

faith a jab to the eye: *but we'll return*
(if only for a day); and some milkweed burns

at the center, a generous magenta heart, enticing
riveted flocks of monarchs to linger. —Twice

I looked the fool to wade that fluid, sink
waist-deep in its accidental colors, thinking

time would stop, thinking the chicory's pilot
blue would flame, a constant across miles,

and lead me toward some wisdom. Foolish? to believe
any of this is other than a sieve

to pour our doubts through, hoping a speck will remain
like a votive lamp against the darkening stain

of effacement—and pierce that final rift
of boundless black that gapes above this gift.

Trilliums

Seeing them, sun-flooded at sunset, their three
ovate leaves paddling out from a single whorl,
their solitary stalks rising into the seraphic
flutter of three green sepals and three
white tongues, I wonder where in the rhizome,
slipped under what mat of its soul
lies the key that trips the lock to door
after door after door. A riven voice sings
through the corridors—*wake-robin, birth-root,
toadshade*—faint incantatory notes like a tonic
chord taken from a dusty hymnal.

Yet paging through the guide I find only the dry
trifling facts regarding, for example, the subtlety
of sexual propagation: that carrion flies
attracted to the gangrenous scent of *Trillium
erectum* ensure its fecundity. But what dictates
this simulacrum of decay, this banishment
of the bee, as if by devilish choice? Survival
by deception implies a mind, and chance
then becomes too casual a guarantee
that the maggot-laced Darwinian kiss
will blossom into certain radiance.

In the *Hours of the Trinity* for Vespers,
pity the Father on His throne of grace, bare-
headed and aggrieved. His arms outstretch so wide
His cope gapes like the cave of space, a vivisected womb.
His splayed fingers scrape the air like rakes

and yet with infinite strength support the cross-
beam where the Son is nailed. Unenviable majesty—
but here, slightly askew within the artist's symmetry
of loss, the Ghost ascends—toward us?—a white flower.
Who, schooled in this myth, even halfheartedly,
if tempted to stoop and pluck, wouldn't cower?

I took a single prime example, and for three days
it graced the chapel of my desk where I'd propped it
in a fluted milk-glass pulpit. The broad leaves
draped like post-pentecostal vestments.
I wish I could say it spoke to me of mysteries,
that the anthers' yellow dust fell across these words
from a firmament I'd never glimpsed before.
But this evening, whatever mitochondrial force
had held such delicate sway ceased its discourse
with the air. Each leaf and sepal curled irredeemably
back from a scorched tip, and the petals, once so tri-

umphantly white, drooped like a bell-less jester's cap.

Plenitude

It always pains me—this abundance
that gems the orchard, this gumdrop excess
against the eyepopping blue of October.

This year the lanes gleam windfall slick,
appling the air. Each footstep adds a hiss
of enticement. Whole families have gathered here,

some nimbling up the branches, straining
for the last, crisp Macs, or hobbling bushel-heavy
down the hillside, hauling their winter's store.

This is the curse, the knowledge of endless
more and more—the tart and sweet
promise—there for the taking.

Spring Peepers

Hyla crucifer

Half-awakened by their calls eastering
      up from the pond's thawing mud,
I imagine a hatch has opened on a hold,
on rare cargo winching toward light.

After their long dream of dreamlessness
      under luffed black sails,
after months of dead reckoning through
clamped silences of ice, they're home.

A thousand steeples chime incessantly
      as the nave of my sleep fills with peeping
choirs—the unbounded Jubilate of frogs.
All next day I hurry the hours till dusk,

eager for another waking. I inch
      my window wider to the dark
and wait for the first to begin. . . . but what I hear—
then cannot shake—rising from their pond's

black throat, rings through the night bringing
      only the saddest wisdom to the world,
a brief imperative, a cry wrenched
from all the nights to come and sent aloft
      for no one but themselves.

At the Cove

Above the first pools
at the continent's wrack
and tatter, we waited

for the moon to swell
like a bud against the black,
and break—then saw

crisp folds of the eternal
sleeper's blanket heave
into seethe and clatter. Love,

I whispered, hold me,
make the world strain and groan
before it grinds us down.

Isolation Ward

I'd brought him hothouse orchids,
        a clutch of purple
dendrobiums, not expecting barricades
        against infection, the doors'
pneumatic *psshh* before the penetralia
        where they'd put him.
Odorless fractals, waxen, strung like lamps
        for a Lenten devotion—*God,*

I thought, *forgive me this gift.* The room
        cried for wildness. I mustn't
talk now of his body, how it would never rise
        from the motored bed,
or speak of my heart's tight purse.
        When I entered, masked
and gowned, he was asleep. How infinite
        that too-near-

to-incorruptible space in which he lay:
        Sleek in its Mies van der Rohe
efficiency, sound-insulated with dual
        unopenable panes overlooking
the radiant bloodflow of city traffic, the room
        hovered like a star
long-accustomed to swallowing worlds.
        Can you blame me

for wanting to louver my gaze past
        the venetian blinds, away
from the gibbeted bags above him,
        dripping their measured tokens

of compassion? What could I give
        but those flowers in their shatterable
flute of glass on the sill, that stood like sentinels
        barring retreat through the gate?

I wish then I could have summoned unpickable
        splendors for him, names
he would have known—like *lobelia cardinalis,*
        gaudy as Pentecostals receiving tongues
of fire. Like bird-on-the-wing. Names
        he'd taught me, which I only now
recover, for what is soiled and lives
        in its place in glory.

On Lexington Avenue

A tapestry hung on stone—
this florist's shop in winter.
The tiered colors disdain
what lies beyond the window.

Millefleurs: their tie
to seasons, lost; their stems,
pared from place. A floating
world where one expects

a unicorn and virgin's face.
The door is locked. A petal
drops like shivered glass
as all the clocks restart.

III

Emily Dickinson in Boston, 1864–65

. . . the calls at the Doctor's are painful, and dear Vinnie,
I have not looked at the Spring.
—E.D. from Cambridge, May 1864

That daguerreotype, with its strabismic gaze,
skews my understanding of her miracle years,
when all heaven seemed to spin on her lathe
and the work fell solid, by the hundreds.

All her life she'd slowly been shutting doors,
until striding home one day through a spume
of widow's lace (or loosestrife or asters)
she'd had enough, then turned the lock, like so,

and doffed her wide-brimmed hat without a flourish.
But what did it mean to elect the white austerities,
to know the world through an atlas circumscribed
and limned on a bedroom's frost-etched panes,

to spar each day with "that little god with epaulettes"
and win? The niceties of legend blanch against the plate:
Her right eye pins us to the paradox of serenity
(how long did she have to hold that pose?); the left eye

strays to confront some hidden radiance—a terror,
she later called it—lurking on vision's periphery.
Symptoms: Foci out of sync, solids ghosted,
the gentlest lights clinging like burrs, ciliary shudders,

all the small betrayals plus that final voltage:
whole foundries of print smeared across the page. Surely
more than panic spurred her into poetry's rolling fires
for those three years. . . . But strolling here, toward dusk,

through the Public Garden—past the swan boats
nuzzling their piers, among the quiet, bivouacked flocks
hoarding the last fugitive rays—I want to imagine her,
here, sure-footed, beyond the squinched regime

of her doctor's care, beyond the clotted vacancies
of the Charles, come to this shadowed calm, this willed
clarity among the geraniums' percussive reds, and yet
it's dislocated fear I sense—a blur—and hurry on.

Odonata

Eye-stitcher, Ear-cutter, Darner.
Perhaps the unenhanced stubbornness

of the protoform engenders this fear,
how the eons have wrought nothing

but their exquisite miniaturization, down
from meter-wide Paleozoic fossils.

Beryl-rods, lapis-sticks—small comforts:
They've still the savage-seeming jaws, the outsized

heads arrayed like NORAD radar domes
attuned to every tic. But perhaps what we fear

the most is admitting the thousand cells
of their compound eyes—those prismatic shards

polished and fixed in Fibonacci strands
a quarter billion years ago—can cast

a mosaic us across the hidden sancta
of their minds. *Flying adder, Blue dragon,*

Devil's-butcher. How better to apprehend
such frightful mastery of the world, make sense

of the fact our miraculous centuries pale
beside the membranous haze and mullions

of these primitive wings? *Globe-skimmer,*
Gauze-hawk, Measuring-stick. Our litanies

swarm up above the pond, tentative mayflies, brief
atonements, wheeling around a definition.

From Hawthornden Castle

Midlothian, Scotland

I've always dreaded this kind of dislocation—the body
popped from its socket, the mind unhoused into the ex-
ile of travel, comfort reduced to the solid gray
dimension of an American Tourister. And yet

I've come to this sturdy sandstone house
to write for a month with a pen dipped in the deep
well of a "laird's retreat." All about me's a jumble:
the upper storey, a Victorian Gothic addendum

atop the sensible Scottish manse which Drummond
appended to an ancienter, ruined keep—
now all rust in this evening's light. Such extravagant
confusion: Heart's-ease and bee hum underfoot,

trills from the yew-tops, the sooty cough of rooks
wheeling overhead, and one questioner somewhere
hunkering in the shadows—*Who? Who?* Must I
unshape myself and turn a different hue to say

I belong here, within these ochre walls? In Hamburg once
I saw stones like these, color of sun-dried blood:
fire-scarred St. Nicholas Church, bombed out
and left in memory. The sky that day was hollow,

dreadful as a bell that would deafen anyone
who strained at the rope again. But here, what tenacious
swagger it would take for a janitor's son to lay claim
to everything he sees, this dragon's hoard of history

atop the glen. Better to make this moment of arrival
a departure too. Even as the stones deepen
through ineffable shades, this wondrous present
is hardening into the familiar, a home, from which a life

can snail forward, an illusion of calm, like this light
that's slowly draining skyward, yielding everything
that matters, a spiral of days I can learn to bear
upon my back, with words (now pray) my hoist and mortar.

Little Homages

1.

Dear one, I deduce I'm drunk	δέδυκε
in the sweet afterrain of May	μὲν
The moon's gone	ἀ σέλαννα
the Pleiades too (if ever	καὶ Πληΐαδες
they were there this night)	μέσαι δὲ νύκτες
I'm lying in dark hours	παρὰ δ' ἔρχετ' ὤρα
lying alone like you	ἔγω
I'm alone in this long dark	δὲ μόνα
but blessing you.	κατεύδω

2.

A black horse with a golden head
is tethered to the stars. The night's
his ample stable. Whatever meaning

        I derive is stitched from random
        flecks. But the moon sails up,
        and I can see the clouds are scripted

                like words beneath his hooves.
                When he shivers in his dreams,
                the equipoise of heaven hums.

3.

All night this primal dance, the improbable
tambourines, the asthmatic trombone
in the flue, the roof-joists groaning
like Atlas. All night these crumpled bits,
this words-brew stirred and steaming
in the room, this half-life
between the dark and dreaming.

And now a muzzy sun staggers up
through slag, and the pavement's sogged
with confetti cut from some Book of Kells.
A morning of lost limbs and high
hysterical trees. And a thrashing viper
at the door, spitting its hiss
of skeptical music.

Invitation to a New Year

Glassed in, here at the edge
of my stony Atlantic, come watch
the opposites commingle and expire—
the braidings of chimneys, sea-wraiths
tangoing till extinction—and let
the raveled years unthread.

Let's recompose the world's clatter—
as something late and Larkinesque.
But ah, the burden of this light, ice
fallen from the eaves, the brittle fire
of that promised star. Yet come,
let's clear the path.

Broth

Some days we cannot help
but stand, chilled to the marrow,
and so let the water brim
with whatever bits we find at hand,
then ease into the kettle the wrecked keel
of a chicken—how like an alchemist
anyone intent on making soup.

The onion, halved then quartered,
separates into a lifetime
of crescent moons, and the carrot's
bright disks float like so many risings
gathered into a single day. Precise,
but not precise. It's not so much practice
as instinct to know that six

peppercorns are enough to pique
the senses, or that a trickle
of salt, rolled from the palm, honors
the one that bore us and will swallow
us again. Somehow we learn
that the parsley must be bitter
as the earth after Eden and one smatter

of thyme is enough to soothe the soul.
We do not think twice about adding
the bay leaf with its tincture of poison.
When we ache, we'll gladly shiver
to stir the broth, then sip, trusting
in the delicate balance of the common-
place to exact the cure.

Constable's Cloud Studies

After the first, when he saw the earth
had poured away like sand, he must have felt a tug,
the heady rush, as he craned his neck and only
      his brush remained, rooted here,

      recording what transpired as "natural
history of the skies." Soon he was mist
burning off from the meadows of the Stour,
and he heard a language sweeping through

the disorderly gradations, something sibylline
      despite the ordinariness
of English weather, those banks of summer
showers, the turbulence and calm, the risks

of plain old days—all that Suffolk lavished
panel upon panel in transcendent
      repetition: (no two alike)
these convolvuli of simplest blues and whites.

In the Moment

before the stone, now in high mid arc,
hits the black static of the lake,
I wait in the uncreated dark
of whatever impulse makes
me want to disrupt that calm.
An empty hand lingers overhead,
a forefinger limp as Adam's, an arm
still in a lame salute to heaven. Instead
of keel-breasted mallards plowing out,
away from their waking past, toward a future tearing
like a seam before them, a blank without
tremor confronts me. It mirrors nothing, stares
passively deep as a dead shark's eye.
The stone's a zero, too, an illusory weight-
lessness, hanging like a star gone out in the sky,
a mere memory of what it was to scintillate
in time. But now, now it moves, and I can see
that flex shake the rigor mortis of eternity.

Even in the Touch

If, as the superstitious claim, the dead
return—not as grainy ectoplasm

served up on photographic plates, but
substantial—shouldn't we conjure them out

of the stuff of this world—not like salamanders
from a flaming log, but seek them

in unbewitching naves: in the less
sanctified bread, in its blossom

of mold, the bitter disappointment
on the tongue; in the things we apprehend

burgeoning where we least want them:
the ring of mushrooms on the lawn,

feared as poison; the polypores latched
like shelves in the orchard; the clutch

of aphids sipping at roses; even in the touch
of the harvestman—there—spindling across your foot?

For if we stub them out, preferring the emerald
lawn, the unspoilt bread, the perfect

apple and bud, haven't we already, love,
stepped across that threshold, never to return?

Valentines

These chain-
  links of consonants,
    these voweled webs among
      love's avowals & our yearn-
        ing's twisting *whys* are but
          the s(y)naps(e) of passion
            played out in air—thrummed
              m's of empathy arcing out of darkness,
            plosive jolts of intention—by which
          we divide our quizzic lives in
        twenty-sixths & formulate,
      reformulate (because we
    never get it right) the
  heart's syntac-
tic curve.

Geological Survey

Caressing your cheek, I note each knuckle
of my hand's become a gullied mesa

scarping down to small blue Coloradoes,
and biceps which once rippled

into elevations of light like a Tuscan
vineyard, now roll in low abandoned meadows.

So much rides the air that would un-
shape us: angry breath and tears, siroccos

of desire, the seasons' freeze then thaws.
And yet, on the revised map of me—

and you—though whole expanses
have eroded, seem unfit for cultivation,

some inexplicable tectonic shift still
exerts itself, renews a landscape that endures.

Brueghel's Harvesters

Though they stoop and sweat
outside a stingy circle
that the pear tree affords . . .

though the mustardy sheaves
of their morning's labor
lie stiff in their ranks as battle-

tallied dead . . . and though
the tree itself, coiling
ungracefully heavenward, past

a blue steeple, splits
their world with its axis,
here is Eden after all

which the artist makes
us contemplate
by planting in the foreground

that husky, unkempt reaper
with his legs splayed wide,
forcing our gaze crotchward,

to the solid drowse
of his codpiece so casually
unlaced, while another,

nearby, holding summer-
ripe fruit firmly to his lips,
stares out at us, and eats.

Ant World: The Leaf-Cutters

Cross-sectioned and cubed,
their "world" had dark, high-
sided glass, like a diorama,
through which we peered
into layered galleries alive
with a kind of vascular flow,

or rather, the well-trafficked
arteries of unrelenting
commerce, leading deeper
through low-heavened pastures
and tiny fungus gardens,
but then rising from this tank

was a single braid,
like a predetermining strand
of DNA, that the curators had rigged
around the room to entice the eye,
like something out of Aesop,
a diversionary skyway meant to teach

a straightforward lesson: thousands
at any time were marching up and out
along this rope, seeking the essential
mulch of their agriculture,
marching for miles, it seemed,
until the rope descended again,

to a table heaped with blossoms
past their prime (the refuse,
I suspected, of some funeral parlor)
where the ants rustled through bolts

of color, merchants among silks,
the sheer excess of them

no louder than a tailor's scissors
until they'd raised a pageant
of banners and joined again
the beginningless procession up
and back along the path they'd come—
so single-mindedly piecemeal

leaf bit by leaf bit.

A Tetradrachm of Alexander the Great

How many days' wages, how many loaves and brimming
kylikes this coin represented for the grunts in
his command I cannot say, but for sheer heft this now
useless ounce of the universal currency plops
in the palm with the undiminished weight of a youth-
king's argentine indifference—a profile struck in high
relief, the polished cheek barely hinting at a beard.

What exactly was the bony socket of his eye
trained on, unblinking, beyond the coin's circumference
where the virtuous abstractions of space must be filled
with history? If not crowns, what Herculean prize?
The lion's pelt already seems to have devoured
most of his head in myth. The mane flares back from his face
like a comet prefiguring change. Which legacy

should we envy: Persepolis in flames, the pickled
corpse enshrined as every petty tyrant's golden boy,
the squabbling brood of princelings with a pie? Nothing's left
but vague reverberations, mere tactical lessons
of a genius at war—and this untarnished bit, which
slaves, chained to a forge, hammered from the molten mass of
his aesthetic. The hand chills at the chance to grasp it.

Snorkeling

Because I want the coral's
ecdysiastic feathered dance
there, lingering within reach,
a few feet beyond the thin oval
mist of my breath, I'll let, if I must,
its kindred's fiery sting graze
my thigh. I'll welcome the welts
of awareness from unwanted things,
the bullet eyes of barracuda
flexing into light, their switch-
blade flesh before me an instant,
then jetting back to fathomable dark. .

Because I want the Delft-blue
parrot fish, schooled as they are
now, in a single sinuous stream,
pouring through this live canyon
while the bony plates of their mouths
grind and remake the reef as they go,
I'll pretend, despite the bellows-
wheeze of lungs, I'm denizen
to this world in which I seem
to hang from the mercurial
sky by a narrow thread—
so vulnerably—and follow them.

Butterfly Farm

A bit absurd perhaps—these exotica of steam-
ing jungles under the artifice of a Quonset sky

but they know no better, content to flit the narrow
air and sip through straws the sweet decay

of citrus rind the "farmer" leaves for them,
or mate in mid-air and dot the hothouse

flora with indiscriminate progeny—
and yet we succumb to the paradisiacal

gaud and glitter of them winging everywhere:
their lepid latticing and iridescent powders

fired like oxides to the extremes of blue
and green, the cryptic Greekness

of their names hinged to the near-
forgotten mythos of meaning—*morpho,*

helicon, kallima—kited in this fragile space
for our delight. How else could we hold

the wholeness of them, the ephemeral
lesson of their lives?

The Book Cover

I hadn't expected to find that fourth-grade book
buried among the random hoard of things
I keep. But there it lay, in the silverfish dark
of a backroom closet between some brittling
Marvel Comics, alluringly Pandoric in its plain,
but creased brown cover. How the leaves creaked
open in my hands to reveal the pious dust
of poems! The unstilled pulse of their meters!
All the childhood greats dragooned and marching
beneath the banner of a bishop's imprimatur—
safe for Catholic schools. Poor catechized child
that I was, I can still set my rusty rote of Keats
cranking: *To know the change and feel it,*
When there is none to heal it . . .
which seems downright ungodly to me now.
But that prophylactic cover, more suggestive
of porn than prosody, fanned out across
my palms like rank petals and set free
again two pent-up, feuding ghosts.

That far September, my mother in her housedress
worked at the kitchen table to save us
a nickel, scissoring a cover from a grocery bag
she would have used for garbage. I sensed
the risk and should have, too, the arrogance
of that nun, rigid with a pride I know now
only avowed poverty can engender, who ordered
all books be covered with the crested, laminate
sheets that only the sisters sold. With that stiff-
spined book before me, its printer's ink fresh-
scented with a hint of bread, I sat upright

ready for Sister William's inspection . . .
and feel again the sting of that woman's slap
to rebuke my mother's handiwork. Who refused
to strip the cover away—this demotic
brown—the wonder of it—like stable hay?
Unchanged, it keeps unfouled that half-
forgotten floor where healing words stammered
and yet were born.

Notes

"Marginalia": The illumination described in the third stanza can be found in *The Hours of Catherine of Cleves* (George Braziller, 1966, plate 23).

"Wood Ducks at Yaddo": In 1899, following the deaths of their four young children, Katrina and Spencer Trask decided to establish Yaddo, their lavish summer house in Saratoga Springs, NY, as a working community for artists and writers. After Spencer was killed in a train accident in 1909, Katrina lived until her death in 1922 in a smaller house on the estate to save money toward fulfilling their plan.

"Holyrood Abbey": Though the twelfth-century abbey was largely destroyed during the Reformation and the turmoil surrounding John Knox, the nave continued to serve as a parish church and burial place for two more centuries, until the vault collapsed in 1768 during a storm.

"The Traffic Between": The epigraph (from *Inferno,* Canto III) refers to Dante's decision to remain silent rather than risk angering Virgil with his questions about why the souls gathered around them seem eager to be ferried by Charon into Hell.

"Poe in the Bronx": I am indebted to Kenneth Silverman's *Edgar A. Poe* (HarperCollins, 1991).

"Trilliums": The "Throne-of-Grace Trinity" appears as plate 38 in *The Hours of Catherine of Cleves* (George Braziller, 1966).

"Isolation Ward": *In memoriam Robert Savage 1951–1993.*

"Emily Dickinson in Boston, 1864–65": Dickinson's move into seclusion at the Homestead in Amherst was gradual, marked by no single compelling event—contrary to my mythmaking assertion in the second stanza. However, beginning in September 1861, Dickinson's congenital eye troubles—thought by some biographers to be strabismus (specifically, walleye, which is evident in the famous daguerreotype of 1848)—worsened to such a degree that Dickinson may have feared she was going blind. Her increased seclusion at this time may have its cause in hypersensitivity to light. In a letter of April 1862 to Thomas Higginson, she mentions a "terror—since September—I could tell none—and so I sing, as the Boy does by the Burying Ground—because I am afraid." Thus began Dickinson's three most productive years of "singing"—over 680 poems brought to completion. Only afterwards did she seek medical treatment from the eminent Cambridge ophthamologist Dr. Henry W. Williams. Though she spent eight abject months in Boston during 1864 under his care, her letters are few at this time and the details of her ailment go unmentioned. "Emily may not be able as she was, but all she can, she will," she wrote to her sister Vinnie in November 1864. "I have been sick so long I do not know the Sun." She traveled to Boston in 1865 for additional treatment, but after returning home in October she seldom left the Homestead again.

"Odonata": The various folk names of dragonflies used in the poem, except for a few of my own variations, can be found in *Dictionary of American Regional English* (Belknap/Harvard University Press).

"From Hawthornden Castle": Built atop Bronze Age caves in the fifteenth century as a fortress, "cavern'd Hawthornden" (as Sir Walter Scott called it) was already in ruins when the poet and historian William Drummond began his restorations in 1638 to create for himself a house of "honest leisure." Drue Heinz, who bought the estate in 1982, reestablished it as a writers' retreat.

"Little Homages": Sappho's lines translate as "Down sink the moon and Pleiades; it's the middle of the night and the hours are going, but I lie here alone." Part 2 was inspired by a watercolor based on the works of William Blake. Part 3 echoes the closing lines of Wallace Stevens' "Sad Strains of a Gay Waltz."

"Ant World: The Leaf-Cutters": Entomologists credit leaf-cutter ants, not human beings, with first developing agriculture.

Acknowledgments

I wish to thank the editors of the following publications in which these poems, some in earlier versions and with different titles, first appeared:

American Literary Review: "From Hawthornden Castle";

The Atavist: "Tulips";

Boulevard: "An Absurdity";

The Chattahoochee Review: "Poe in the Bronx";

Connecticut Review: "Emily Dickinson in Boston, 1864–65";

The Gettysburg Review: "Even in the Touch," "Odonata";

Green Mountains Review: "Broth," "Cantus";

The Greensboro Review: "Millennial Song," "Plenitude";

The Kenyon Review: "Autumn Nightfall," "The White Orchids";

New Orleans Review: "Isolation Ward," "Judas Trees";

North Atlantic Review: "Ant World: The Leaf-Cutters," "Marginalia";

Pendragon: "On Lexington Avenue";

Pivot: "A Rogue Wave";

Poet Lore: "Barberry," "Little Homages," "Nettle," "Northern Lights";

Poetry: "The Book Cover," "The Clearing," "Constable's Cloud Studies," "The Failure of Similes," "Fiddleheads," "Geological Survey," "Holyrood Abbey," "Icebound," "In the Moment," "A Tetradrachm of Alexander the Great," "Valentines";

Poets On: "The News";

Riversedge: "Garden After Frost," "The Rock Doves," "Snorkeling," "The Vacant Lot";

Shenandoah: "Trilliums," "Wood Ducks at Yaddo";

Slant: "Remembering the Garden";

The Southern Review: "Butterfly Farm";

Southwest Review: "Masks";

Sycamore Review: "Brueghel's Harvesters";

Tar River Poetry: "The Traffic Between";

Traffic Report: "Spring Peepers".

"Invitation to a New Year" was first published as a limited edition by Steve Miller of Red Hydra Press, © 1993.

"At the Cove" was first published as a broadside by Red Hydra Press, © 1996.

I am grateful to the National Endowment for the Arts for a Creative Writing Fellowship that greatly assisted me during the writing of this book. I also wish to thank the Hawthornden Castle International Retreat for Writers, the Virginia Center for the Creative Arts, and the Corporation of Yaddo for their nurturing support during my residencies there. I thank, too, Michael Waters for his critical eye and friendship; Jeanne Braham and Roger Lathbury, two pillars; and Sonia Raiziss and Al Poulin, sustainers always in memory.

About the Author

Richard Foerster is the author of two previous poetry collections, *Sudden Harbor* and *Patterns of Descent*, both published by Orchises Press. He has received many fellowships and awards for his poetry, including the "Discovery"/*The Nation* Award, *Poetry* magazine's Bess Hokin Prize, a 1995 fellowship from the National Endowment for the Arts, and a 1997 Individual Artist Fellowship from the Maine Arts Commission. He edits the literary magazine *Chelsea* and lives in York Beach, Maine.

BOA EDITIONS, LTD.: AMERICAN POETS CONTINUUM SERIES

Vol. 1   *The Fuhrer Bunker: A Cycle of Poems in Progress*
W. D. Snodgrass

Vol. 2   *She*
M. L. Rosenthal

Vol. 3   *Living With Distance*
Ralph J. Mills, Jr.

Vol. 4   *Not Just Any Death*
Michael Waters

Vol. 5   *That Was Then: New and Selected Poems*
Isabella Gardner

Vol. 6   *Things That Happen Where There Aren't Any People*
William Stafford

Vol. 7   *The Bridge of Change: Poems 1974–1980*
John Logan

Vol. 8   *Signatures*
Joseph Stroud

Vol. 9   *People Live Here: Selected Poems 1949–1983*
Louis Simpson

Vol. 10   *Yin*
Carolyn Kizer

Vol. 11   *Duhamel: Ideas of Order in Little Canada*
Bill Tremblay

Vol. 12   *Seeing It Was So*
Anthony Piccione

Vol. 13   *Hyam Plutzik: The Collected Poems*

Vol. 14   *Good Woman: Poems and a Memoir 1969–1980*
Lucille Clifton

Vol. 15   *Next: New Poems*
Lucille Clifton

Vol. 16   *Roxa: Voices of the Culver Family*
William B. Patrick

Vol. 17   *John Logan: The Collected Poems*

Vol. 18   *Isabella Gardner: The Collected Poems*

Vol. 19   *The Sunken Lightship*
Peter Makuck

Vol. 20   *The City in Which I Love You*
Li-Young Lee

Vol. 21   *Quilting: Poems 1987–1990*
Lucille Clifton

Vol. 22   *John Logan: The Collected Fiction*

Vol. 23   *Shenandoah and Other Verse Plays*
Delmore Schwartz

Vol. 24   *Nobody Lives on Arthur Godfrey Boulevard*
Gerald Costanzo

Vol. 25   *The Book of Names: New and Selected Poems*
Barton Sutter

Vol. 26   *Each in His Season*
W. D. Snodgrass

Vol. 27   *Wordworks: Poems Selected and New*
Richard Kostelanetz

Vol. 28   *What We Carry*
Dorianne Laux

Vol. 29   *Red Suitcase*
Naomi Shihab Nye

Vol. 30   *Song*
Brigit Pegeen Kelly

Vol. 31   *The Fuehrer Bunker: The Complete Cycle*
W. D. Snodgrass

Vol. 32   *For the Kingdom*
Anthony Piccione

Vol. 33   *The Quicken Tree*
Bill Knott

Vol. 34   *These Upraised Hands*
William B. Patrick

Vol. 35   *Crazy Horse in Stillness*
William Heyen

Vol. 36   *Quick, Now, Always*
Mark Irwin

Vol. 37 *I Have Tasted the Apple*
         Mary Crow

Vol. 38 *The Terrible Stories*
         Lucille Clifton

Vol. 39 *The Heat of Arrivals*
         Ray Gonzalez

Vol. 40 *Jimmy & Rita*
         Kim Addonizio

Vol. 41 *Green Ash, Red Maple,*
         Black Gum
         Michael Waters

Vol. 42 *Against Distance*
         Peter Makuck

Vol. 43 *The Night Path*
         Laurie Kutchins

Vol. 44 *Radiography*
         Bruce Bond

Vol. 45 *At My Ease: Uncollected Poems*
         of the Fifties and Sixties
         David Ignatow

Vol. 46 *Trillium*
         Richard Foerster

Colophon

Trillium, poems by Richard Foerster, has been typeset using
Monotype Dante and Arabesque fonts, as well as LaserGreek
Graeca, and issued in a first edition of 1,250 copies,
of which 1200 trade copies are bound in paper.

Twenty-five copies for sale to the trade are bound
in quarter cloth and French papers over boards, numbered I–XXV,
signed by the poet, and include a poem in holograph
by Richard Foerster.

An additional twenty-five copies, also bound in quarter cloth
and French papers over boards, are numbered i–xxv,
signed by the poet, and reserved
for presentation purposes.